Flower Power

by

Barbara Barber

G Charney
BOOKS

© Barbara Barber, 1999

G Charney Publications
Ramridge Dene, Ramridge Park,
Weyhill, Andover, Hants SP11 0QP
Tel: 01264 772465

U.S.A. Distributor
Quilters' Resource
P. O. Box 148850, Chicago, IL 60614
Tel: 1-800-676-6543   Fax: 1773-278-1348

ISBN 0 9530848 1 7

Design by Colin Currill Creative Services

Printed in England by KNP Group Ltd

Front Cover and Title Page Illustration:
CATS,
87" x 87" by Barbara Barber,
Hampshire, England
Photo courtesy of The Patchwork Association,
P. O. Box 300, Hethersett, Norwich, Norfolk NR9 3DB.

Back Cover Illustration:
Goato and Friends,
83" x 83" by Barbara Barber, Hampshire, England
Collection of the Museum
of the American Quilter's Society,
Paducah, Kentucky, USA.
Photo courtesy of the American Quilter's Society.

CONTENTS

To my brother, David Ploug,
with love.

ACKNOWLEDGMENTS

Quilters are wonderful people and I thank all of those who have enriched my quilting experiences, many of whom will never know how they have touched my life and work.

I thank Julie Standen for all her hard efforts and the beautiful work which resulted.

I thank Margaret Docherty for her contribution and the many amusing conversations we have in the name of friendship.

I thank Linda Park for her contributions and continuous enthusiastic help and support.

I thank Chris Gibson Barnfather for her mental creativity which she willingly shares with me.

I thank June Thorpe for a very special friendship which has been of great value to me during the writing of this book, as it always has been over the years.

I thank my daughter Eliza very much for her help and especially for her understanding tolerance.

I thank my husband Peter for all he does that makes my life complete and always being willing and able to lend a helping hand.

I thank Colin Currill for all his technical help, for doing a super job and making things seem easy. Also, for maintaining a splendid sense of humour throughout and, as always, being a pleasure to work with.

INTRODUCTION

This is a book all about the magical power of flowers. Most people love flowers in one form or another. They are one of nature's ways of putting on a pretty show. I sometimes ponder a very solemn thought - what if we lived in a world which had no flowers?

In my quilts Goato & Friends and CATS, flowers play a major part in the overall design. All of the flower patterns in this book, except for one, come from those two quilts. They are my own original designs except for one which my daughter drew and three which my husband drew. In the very beginning, faced for the first time with this type of design work, I looked to other sources such as gardening books and other art forms for inspiration. However, after drawing several of them I purposely tried to avoid any outside input. Gardening books presented me with ideas which were too realistic to easily sew and also I became hooked on the fun and excitement of making up my own.

You will notice that my flowers are not the cut variety but are more like little plants. I call them "plantlets". Hardly any of the designs are based on real flowers - I'm afraid I wouldn't be very good at that sort of thing. Instead, they are stylised and let the imagination run free. This also gives the freedom to use colour in ways that might even make Mother Nature think once or twice.

The flowers on my quilts were created by using machine appliqué techniques. I have included basic instructions for the type of machine appliqué that I use in my work. Don't limit your imagination to this use only. A great number of the designs are suitable for hand appliqué. Others can be very simply modified to make them suitable for this technique. The same goes for quilting patterns. They would make lovely and very personalised greeting cards. You can use the flowers as they have been drawn or take various elements from several different ones to concoct a new one. And best of all, after looking through the flowers you will be itching to get creating.

This book is intended mainly as a pattern source book and also to convince the many skeptics that say "I can't draw" that they most certainly can produce wonderful and original designs themselves. This is exactly what I used to think but several hundred flower designs later, I feel certain that if I can do it, you can too.

Until I got started on the flowers in Goato & Friends, I had no idea how very much fun it would be. By the time I made CATS, I was actually looking forward to the flowers with eager anticipation. I've enjoyed my work with flowers and truly hope you do, too. Most of all, I hope that the power of flowers will make you smile.

Goato & Friends - 83" x 83" - Barbara Barber, Hampshire, England   1995
Collection of the Museum of the American Quilter's Society, Paducah, Kentucky, USA.
Photo courtesy of the American Quilter's Society.

CATS - 87" x 87" - Barbara Barber, Hampshire, England   1998
Photo courtesy of The Patchwork Association.

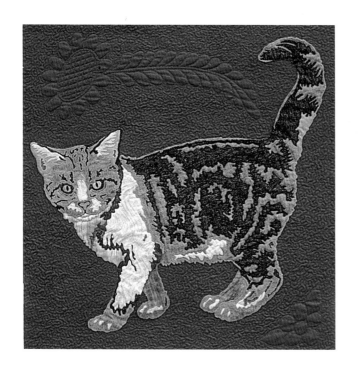

EQUIPMENT MATERIALS and SUPPLIES

My use of the flower designs has, for the most part, been limited to machine appliqué and in this chapter I will review the materials, equipment and supplies that I use when sewing these designs.

Sewing Machine - Any machine which will do a zigzag stitch in variable widths is suitable. Obviously, as with any job, the better the tools, the easier it is to produce a high quality result. On very basic machines some of the machine embroidery stitches which have been used will not be possible. They could, of course be added by hand.

I sew on a Bernina 1260 and will give settings which I have used on this machine. All machines are different and you will have to make trials to ascertain the correct settings for your particular machine. Whilst teaching workshops I have found that machine settings can vary considerably even between two of the same make and model. By giving the settings for my machine, it will give you a starting point for your trial pieces.

Please remember that a clean well-tended machine will always give a better result. Be kind to your machine and it will repay you with trouble-free sewing. I have got into the habit of cleaning it quite thoroughly each time I use a full bobbin. As well as cleaning in the bobbin area, I remove the throat plate and clean this area, too. After cleaning, I apply a tiny amount of oil to the bobbin race. By applying a very, very small amount of oil on a regular basis, it keeps the machine running smoothly and I am not worried about getting those blobs of oil on my fabric which can occur if too much oil is applied at one time.

Machine Needles - The size needle I use for appliqué is a Size 80. If you chose to work in fabrics which are heavier or finer than the standard quilting cottons you would have to reconsider the size of the needle. For this type of appliqué the needle really does need to be sharp in order to prevent skipped stitches from occurring. Change the needle as soon as it shows signs of dulling.

Fusible Web - The type of appliqué I do is a raw-edged method and does not involve turning under the edges of the appliqué pieces. This allows for far more detail to be used than in any other form of appliqué. The edges do need to be stablised and for this I use a fusible web. I do not, however, rely on this web to hold the work together in any way. It is the stitches in the piece that must hold the work securely together and I consider the web to be only a very handy form of basting which will hold the pieces in place while they are stitched. This is because I use a light weight version of the fusible web and do not think that it can be relied upon to securely hold the edges of the appliqué down, without fraying, during washing and wear. I use a light weight version because I want the quilt to remain soft and pliable. There are medium and heavy weight webs which will hold more securely but will also stiffen up the finished piece considerably. There are many name brands available and you must find one that you enjoy using. The brand I like and use still has a draw back and that is that the paper will easily separate from the web before you are ready for it to do so. Careful handing and storage will prevent this to a large degree. If you have bought a yard or two of fusible web do not work on the whole of it at one time. Cut off about 10" at a time to work with as this will eliminate most of the separation problem.

Spray Starch - If you still have not tried spray starch for your quiltmaking then you really should give it a go! I use it on all of the fabrics for almost all of my quilts and would hate to return to the days before I discovered the merits of starch. There simply is no comparison between working with a firm and a flimsy fabric. This is especially true when using my methods of machine appliqué. I do not use a stabliser under the work and by using a very well starched background fabric you will prevent tunneling or ruching as you sew with a zigzag stitch. When I say well starched, I do mean well starched and the more intricate the piece, the stiffer you need to starch. The fabrics which are to be used for the appliqué pieces should also be starched but they do not need quite as much as they will be further stablised with the fusible web before sewing.

I use a spray although you could use a dip starch. The reason for this is simply for convenience. The methods I use to apply the starch changed somewhat during the making of CATS when I needed lots and lots of background fabric in large pieces. It can be difficult, not to mention very tedious, to starch large pieces using the iron to dry out the fabric between the numerous coats which would be necessary to achieve the desired stiffness. The way I do it now requires a little pre-planning but takes all the bother out of it and produces an excellent result. Place a layer of plastic sheeting down on the floor which is several inches larger than the fabric which you plan to starch; I use new black plastic rubbish bin liners. Lay the fabric on top of the plastic and spray with starch until the fabric is completely soaked. If possible do this in a room which gets little use. Leave this overnight to dry out completely. Use a steam iron to turn this into a beautifully firm fabric which is then ready for sewing.

Light Box - This is not an absolute necessity but if you are working with dark or printed background fabrics it will make things alot easier. You do not have to use a light box as such and could start by using a glass table with a lamp placed below it. Another alternative is to place a light in a cardboard box and a piece of glass on top, taking care with the edges of the glass. Commercially made light boxes can be quite expensive and I have yet to see one which I consider to be good value for money . The commercial ones are not only expensive but the ones which I have seen have never been as good as the homemade varieties. There is no doubt that a good light box is a real asset and makes so many aspects of quiltmaking easier, neater and more accurate. If you want to acquire a light box I would suggest that you consider having one made. Many of you will have someone who would be willing or able to build it if you are not able to do so yourself. Even if you have no one to do it, I feel that you would be better off paying a carpenter to make it rather than buying a commercial one. Before making it, try to consider its usage from many angles and hopefully you will end up with a really effective box. Also, it is a very good idea to be sure to make it big enough, in the first instance, to cope with all your quilting needs.

My husband made me a splendid light box and I really would hate to be without it. It is treasured most for the ease with which it lets me do even the most intricate appliqué work without ever marking the background fabric. One of it's other valuable uses is for marking quilting designs onto my quilt tops. It is large and not very pretty but it does the job intended exceedingly well. Peter made it from a double-glazed door panel which measures 26" x 34". He made a timber box which is 6" deep and fitted the glass panel into the top of it. There are two fluorescent light units fitted into the bottom of it. He also gave me the luxury of a switch which means that I do not have to unplug it each time I finish using it. The finished box is very heavy but the glass panel can be easily removed and the bottom moved separately. I hope this gives you some ideas if you are thinking of having one made.

Fabrics - The choice of fabric is up to you but if it is your intention to use the appliqué in a quilt you should choose a good quality fabric. I generally use fabrics which have been specifically made for quilting. The fabrics are always 100% cotton as I know this means I will get a dependably good result. Before using the fabrics in a quilt, I always pre-wash them. For the type of appliqué described in this book you should avoid the use of loosely woven fabrics.

As for colour, it is entirely up to you. The flowers are not meant to resemble real ones and can be made in any colour. If you are working on a group of flowers or including lots of them in a quilt, it is a good idea to select a palette to work from. When working with flower designs, this is really easy. When selecting your fabrics, all you have to do is imagine that you are picking flowers to make a large bouquet. Be sure to use quite a few greens in a wide range of shades. When looking at fabrics, don't just look at colour; texture plays such an important role. A few directional prints will enable you to turn your flowers into something special. Be sure to include different shades of each colour you choose to use. I used over 75 different fabrics for the flowers in CATS with about twenty of them being greens. After you have picked your bunch of fabrics, fan them out over the background fabric. If you like the effect, you are ready to sew. If one keeps catching your eye, remove it and see if you like this better. Sometimes you will feel that the fabrics look nice but lack zing. Try adding a really striking colour and this may be what was missing. The most important thing about colour is to never be afraid of it and to work with the colours that you really enjoy.

Threads - When stitching is utilitarian rather than decorative the best result will be obtained if the thread matches the fabric of the appliqué piece as close as is possible. If it is a decorative stitch then the colour of thread is really up to you.

Scissors - A pair of really good scissors is a necessity for producing work of a high standard. They need to be small, sharp and have fine points which are sharp to the very tips. That does not mean that they have to be a very expensive pair. For the past eight years I have used the same little scissors for all my quilting including cutting paper, fabric, fusible web and thread. They are still in excellent condition and will be used to make many more quilts. I use the 5" needlework scissors by Fiskars and I also have the sharpener made by Fiskars which really does keep the scissors in prime condition. Scissors which are dull or have blunt tips will only lead to frustration.

DRAW YOUR OWN FLOWERS

When it comes to drawing designs freehand, my experience of quilters is that, for the most part, they view it in the same way as I do and say, "I can't draw". That is certainly the way I feel but several hundred flower designs later I have concluded that it really doesn't matter whether I can draw or not. The one thing I do know is that if I had let that fear of having to draw rule the day then I would never have designed a single flower let alone all the others which followed. There is a knack, and practice does make it easier and quicker, but whatever the speed you work at the satisfaction of producing your own original designs will give you a boost and urge you on to try again and again.

The most difficult part is drawing that very first line. After that you can free up more and more and start doodling away with great abandon. The best way to start is with a spiral notepad and pencil. Just start by drawing some shapes for flower heads; they don't have to look good or even like flowers. Just start drawing and drawing, page after page. Some will be pure rubbish and many of mine have made me laugh at just how pathetic they look. In the drawings shown on this page, you can see a few of my many, many rough efforts which eventually led to the flowers in CATS.

once that will be the only time I manage to do it. If it has been rubbed out it is gone forever. Trace the bits you like and alter the areas you don't like.

Once in a while you will really surprise yourself and almost as if by accident, draw something which really pleases you. The more attempts you make, the more chances you have of getting something that you really like. Draw these sketches quickly, one after another, without giving much thought to what you are doing. It takes very little time to quickly and roughly draw many different flower shapes. Do not take the time to erase something if it doesn't work, just move on and try again. If you make a drawing that for the most part you really like, don't be tempted to erase it to alter it. I have often found that if I get something right

After having a go at the flower heads for a while you should start doodling loads of leaf shapes. Again, the more rough shapes you draw, the more useable designs you will end up with. Drawing the stems is easier than you might image. Start by keeping it simple. Draw sets of lines to represent the stems. It really is easier than you think and then you are ready to add flower heads and leaves to the stems. Before you

know it you will be adding buds as well. When I am drawing the stems, I do not worry about the straightness or smoothness of the lines; that can be dealt with later and in any case, the less than perfect look adds to the charm.

All of the above work should be done quickly in pencil. When you come up with a design that you like, it is time to refine it. Think about the methods you will use to sew it and make sure that it works. Now take a fine black marker and trace it onto plain white paper. As you do so, straighten out any kinks or wobbly lines that you want rid of. It is very easy to turn a crude drawing into a good design when tracing it in black ink. Your design is now ready to use.

I do so hope you will try to draw your own designs as it is very satisfying and the more you do it, the more you will want to carry on and the designs will become better and better. I must stress, however, that if you are unwilling to start doodling those rough sketches you are cheating yourself of the fun, the challenge, and the surprise of finding out exactly what you are capable of - even if you can't draw!

MACHINE APPLIQUE

For this type of appliqué, I do not use a satin stitch but rather a slightly open zigzag stitch. I like the effect and it allows me to use a great amount of detail in the work. In this chapter, I will give my methods and you can either use them as they are presented or adapt them to suit your particular needs and tastes.

THE PATTERNS

The patterns presented in this book can be photocopied or traced to make it easy to use them. The spiral binding will allow you to photocopy with ease and accuracy. Remember that you can enlarge or shrink the designs using a photocopier. All of the flower patterns in this book are about 15% larger than the ones I used when making Goato & Friends and CATS. This was done to make them easier to sew but you could, of course, take them back to their original size by reducing them by 15%. All of the patterns have been sized to fit a 6" square which is set diagonally on point.

Figure 2

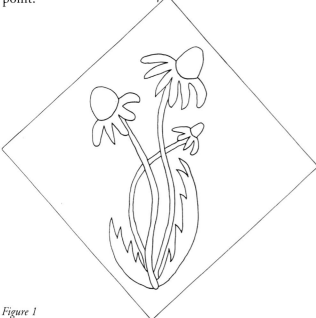

Figure 1

When considering the patterns remember to think about altering them. In *Figure 2*, you can see the drawing of the Rose it as it has been presented on page 78. The stems and leaves are all cut out separately and this allows more opportunity to play with shades of colour.

In *Figure 3*, the stem is cut from just one piece. It is quicker to do it this way and when doing alot of flowers can be nice for a change.

You could take this one step further and cut all the leaves and stems from just one piece as shown in *Figure 4*. I

used this effect in just one design and that was Fire Flower. It can be very effective but requires more care when cutting out.

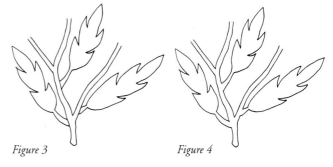

Figure 3   Figure 4

A great deal of fun can be had playing mix and match with the patterns. Take flowers, leaves and stems from three different designs and come up with your own new one.

ORDER OF SEWING

Once you have your prepared pattern you will first need to consider the order of sewing. The easiest way to do that is to look at the drawing of Tulips *(Fig 5)*.

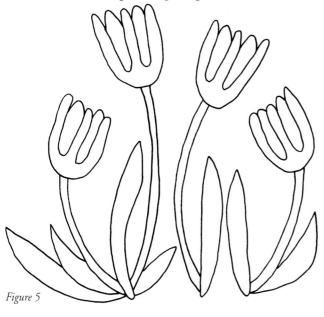

Figure 5

Now look at the following four photographs which show the way the pieces were added to gradually build up and make the complete design.

In *Figure 6*, this design has the pieces numbered to show the order they were added to the background fabric.

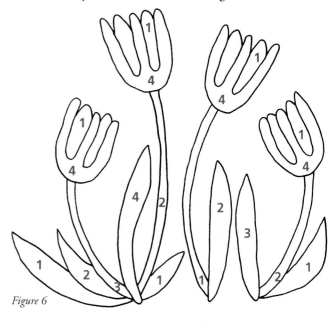

Figure 6

There is an easy way to decide if a piece goes under or over another piece. If a line runs into another line then it must be tucked under the piece it runs into. In *Figure 7*, the lines of the stem run into the line of the leaf. Therefore, the stem would be added first with a seam allowance extending under the leaf.

In *Figure 8*, the lines of the leaf run into the line of the stem. The leaf would be added first with a seam allowance extending under the stem.

By looking at the patterns in this way you can easily decide which pieces should be sewn first. The patterns

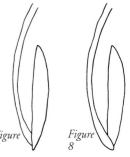

Figure 7   *Figure 8*

FLOWER POWER

in this book have not been numbered because it is not necessary and I do, in fact, use a numbering system in a different way to make things easier. This will be explained later.

Look at various patterns in the book and using the guidelines above, decide on the order for sewing the appliqué pieces.

USING FUSIBLE WEB

Fusible web has a paper coating on it which is peeled off before the appliqué piece is ironed down on to the background fabric. This should not be done until the appliqué piece is ready to be applied to the background. Trace the design parts onto the paper side of the fusible web. The pattern must be turned over or reversed so that you are tracing it from the back of the design. A light box makes this easy but if you do not have a light box then very carefully trace the design through to the wrong side of the paper. Trace each piece of the design separately with little extensions added to the pieces when they lie under another appliqué piece. When tracing patterns I number the pieces and also the original design. These numbers are not given to indicate order of placement but are used as a means of identifying which bits belong to which flower of the drawing and will help you recognise the stems and leaves. This may not seem like it would be a problem but I have found that this helps tremendously because the pieces may not be easy to identify as they have been drawn in reverse. Using my design for Tulips, you can see in *Figure 9* how I would number the pieces.

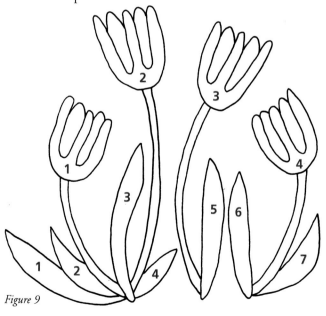

Figure 9

Notice that the flowers are numbered 1 to 4 and the leaves 1 to 7. I would label the stems with the same number as the flower they belong to when tracing them onto the fusible web. In the drawing below you can see some of the pieces for the design just as I would trace them, in reverse with extensions when necessary, onto the paper side of the fusible web.

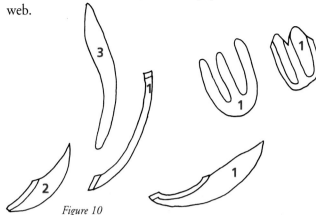

Figure 10

Cut around the tracings roughly, leaving about $^1/_8$" excess right the way around each piece.

Using the fabric of your choice, place the fusible web onto the wrong side of the fabric with the paper side which shows the drawing uppermost. Iron the paper down using a setting for cotton fabrics. The fusible web will melt and adhere to the fabric. Now you can cut the piece out on the traced lines. Be sure to do so accurately as this will make building up the design easier. Also, be sure to include any seam allowances which go under other appliqué pieces. For me, it is important to draw any allowances onto the fusible web when tracing the design because then I can always be sure that I have remembered to include it and that it is of the correct size and shape.

SEWING THE DESIGN

Set your sewing machine to do a zigzag stitch. The settings for my machine are 1.5 for the stitch width and 1 for the stitch length. I also alter the tension setting for the top thread on my machine to about 3. This will loosen the tension of the top thread. The reason for this is because although I may change the top thread many times for a design I use the same bobbin thread throughout. By slackening off the top tension, you prevent the bobbin thread from occasionally coming up to the top and showing a contrasting thread. When I work, the back of the piece shows more of the top thread than it does bobbin thread.

Be sure to do plenty of trial bits before starting to sew on your actual design. Do these trials on fabric which is well

Reverse of Spoon Flower

starched in the same way as the background fabric. If you are going to use machine embroidery stitches, it is always wise to try these out on a trial piece before attempting them on your appliqué work. The two stitches which I have used for machine embroidery on the Bernina 1260 are numbers 16, a type of feather stitch, and 26 which is a blanket or buttonhole stitch. The width and length can be adjusted as you sew to achieve some lovely results. I have also used a straight stitch and a satin stitch.

To position the first pieces to be sewn, turn the pattern back over so that it now faces right side up again. Unless you are using a light coloured background fabric, you will probably have to use a light box or something similar to position the appliqué pieces. Place the pattern onto the light box. Put the background fabric, right side up, on top of the paper design. Remove the paper backing from the back of the first pieces of appliqué. Use the pattern showing through to position the first pieces you want to sew. Carefully move the background fabric to the ironing board and use the iron to attach the pieces on to the background fabric.

Figure 11

See the first step for sewing Tulips in *Figure 11*. The zigzag stitch should be done with almost all of the stitch lying on the appliqué piece; the needle falls just barely off the edge of the appliqué for the outside edge of the stitch. The best result will be obtained by sewing very slowly. Notice that I have not sewn right the way around the yellow centre sections of the tulips but only on the edge which will not be covered by the next fabric. As the beginning and the end of this row of stitches will be covered by the next piece, you can cut off the ends without pulling them to the back and securely knotting them. By looking at that same photograph, you will notice that I have added some

machine embroidery at this stage. The embroidery threads at the outer tips of the leaves will need to be pulled to the back of the work and secured. The embroidery threads at the stem end will be covered by the next line of stitching and can be cut off. After sewing all of the first pieces down repeat the process as I have shown in the construction photographs of Tulips on page 16.

MORE COMPLEX DESIGNS

As with anything you are new to, you should start by doing simple designs and build up to the more complex ones. This will allow you to get a very thorough understanding of the techniques and also to perfect your stitching. In this section I am going to use my design called Spoon Flower, shown on page 21.

Spoon Flower

This is a new design which I have not yet used on a quilt. The technique known as reverse appliqué is used in this design. I really wish I could throw the term "Reverse Appliqué" out the window! It seems to be able to instill more fear in quilters than almost any other term I know of and yet there simply is no mystery to it. It is basically the same as any other form of appliqué and using these machine techniques it is no more difficult to do. The main thing is that you need to understand exactly what you are doing. You are placing one fabric beneath another fabric which has a hole cut out of it. The bottom piece must be larger than the hole so that there is an overlap.

Here you can see the pieces which have the fusible web applied and are cut out ready to make the leaves for the Spoon Flower. On the left, you can see the back of the pieces for one of the leaves. The smaller piece will be placed under the hole which has been cut into the leaf. This is basically reverse appliqué. Notice that there is an allowance added right the way around the small piece.

In this photo you can now see the two leaves as they would be prepared for placement on the background fabric. The one on the right shows what the back would look like. Remove the paper backing from the main part of the leaf. Use the light box to centre the main leaf section over the top of the smaller piece. Use the tip of your iron to "baste"

these two together by carefully touching it with the iron in several places just along the edge of the hole. Remember that the main leaf section now has no paper on it and will stick if the iron touches this section. Remove all the paper backing before positioning the pieces onto the background square.

This shows the first pieces sewn onto the background fabric. Notice that I have used a blanket or buttonhole stitch on the pink bud. When using a decorative stitch to sew on an appliqué piece, be sure to adjust the stitch length so that the stitches are not too far apart. Remember that although these may be decorative they are also functional and must be close enough together to hold the appliqué on securely. I never use a stitch length which is longer than 1.75 for this type of work.

In these photographs, I have added the darker pink section of the bud and am trying out two different stem colours. Notice how the one on the right deadens the effect whilst the one on the left brightens the whole thing and emphasises the details of the leaves and the bud.

Here you can see work in progress on the flower head *(see over)*. First, prepare and cut out the little orange centre section. Next appliqué it on to the fabric that you wish to use as the main flower fabric; my choice was a pink fabric. After stitching the centre piece onto the pink you will cut out the whole flower shape. Trace the design onto the

fusible web in the usual way but be sure to trace the very centre piece as well. Turn the pink fabric over and use the stitching as a guide for placing and ironing the fusible web in position. Now cut out the pink section and appliqué it onto the stem, using the light box to position it.

On the right in the photograph above, you can see the wrong side of the yellow section of the flower. When you have to cut out small holes it is easier if you cut out the holes before cutting around the outside of the piece, particularly on something as complex as this.

Remove the paper backing from the yellow section and position it on top of the flower head. Attach the very centre of the yellow section to the flower by "gluing" it down with the tip of the iron. Use a straight pin to maneuver the

little pieces to be used under the holes in the yellow into the correct place. Secure them with the iron and then stitch. It is often very difficult to decide the right centre for a flower without trying out several. You can see the ones I tried out for this flower at the bottom of the previous column.

On this design, I used some short straight stitches for decorative work and find it gives the best result if two lines of stitching are used. The more you sew these types of designs the more ideas you will come up with to enhance them. Whilst I'm all for the use of machine embroidery, I urge you to use it with caution - it is extremely easy to overdo it.

Spoon Flower

Sunflower - Free Motion Appliqué by Barbara Barber.

Free Motion Appliqué can be used on any of the designs. To do it, drop the feed dog and use a zig-zag stitch setting.

Examples of other ways to use designs by Linda Park, Maryland, USA.

Above - Découpage Tray.   *Below* - Photo Album Cover

GALLERY OF FLOWERS

All of the flowers in this section were sewn for the book by Julie Standen. I am thrilled with the result and deeply grateful to her.

Julie and I first met in 1994. I was teaching a workshop at Country Threads in Bath and Julie was a student. From that first meeting, I not only liked her but also admired and respected her work tremendously. Since that time I have been lucky enough to have Julie in many workshops. She has always been willing to help whenever she can and has contributed to my first book and three of my videos. We were discussing the fact that I was going to do this book and Julie offered to sew the flowers for me. That was an offer too good to refuse as I had just finished making CATS and could not face sewing all those flowers again so soon. I knew her workmanship would be great and I was right. Thank you, Julie!

Julie Standen comes from the Bristol area. She has a demanding career as a personnel officer in the civil service but still finds plenty of time for quiltmaking.

PETER'S FLOWER

This was the first of three flowers that my husband drew for me. Peter has always been very involved in my quilting and it gives me great joy that not only is he interested but is also always willing to lend a hand. Peter is much better at drawing than I am and he tends to approach it from a much more realistic angle.

I know he finds it quite difficult to simplify or stylise things enough to make it possible to sew the design.

See page 103 for pattern.

FIRST FLOWER

This was the first flower I ever drew or stitched in appliqué.
I can recall only too vividly the blank expanse of white paper waiting for me to have the nerve
to make those first rough drawings. After the initial cautious attempts it became easier and a great deal of fun.

See page 104 for pattern.

OCTET

See page 104 for pattern.

POKE FLOWER

In CATS, you can first see this flower along the upper edge of the quilt.
Later, along the right hand edge of that quilt you can see it again, but this time with a different leaf.

See page 105 for pattern.

SUNDIAL

This was the second flower that Peter drew for me. Although I was very grateful for the design and I love the flower, I never thanked him much whilst I was sewing it. It's not particularly difficult but it is rather tedious.

See page 105 for pattern.

HOT CROSS BUN FLOWER

It may be an unlikely name but that is how I saw it right from the beginning.

See page 106 for the pattern.

FANFARE

The flower head on this design is highly stylised and as it was one of my earliest,
probably had input from Jacobean embroidery designs.
I have found that as this design is far removed from any living flower, you can really have fun with the colours.

See page 107 for pattern.

LAZY DAISY

Apparently, the missing petals on the left hand flower head bothered Julie Standen's husband
as she sewed this sample for me. Why they were left off in the first instance I'm not sure.
If it bothers you as well, simply add a few more petals.

See page 108 for pattern.

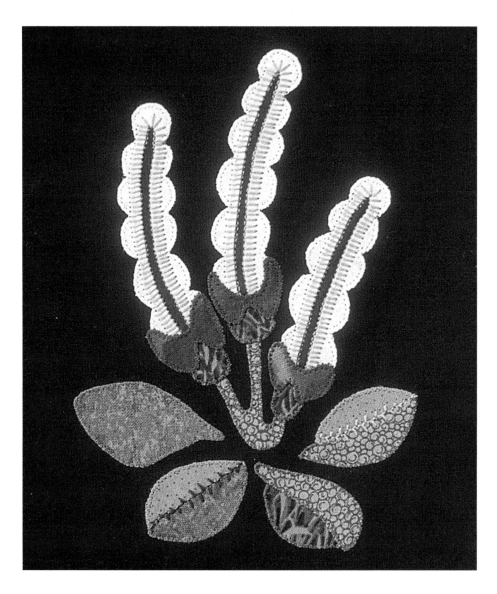

CANDLEWICK

This is not a flower for the beginner to tackle but is, in fact, a great deal of fun to sew.

See page 108 for the pattern.

BOTTLEBRUSH

Sometimes one design inspires another and this was the case with Bottlebrush.
After making Candlewick, shown on the previous page, I added some bits to it and changed the leaves.
See page 109 for the pattern.

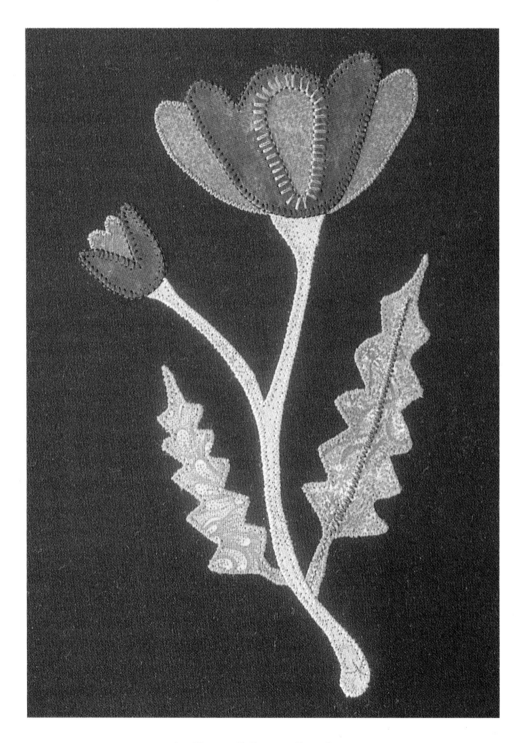

BUTTERCUP

The jagged edges of the leaves could be smoothed out or at least softened to make for easier sewing.
See page 109 for the pattern.

HOUND'S TOOTH

I first used this one in the dog block of Goato & Friends. As I was making the little white petals for that block,
I came to think of them as teeth - hence the name. It was also used in the goat block.
On Goato & Friends, it was made with a plain leaf but by the time I used it twice in CATS,
I had added a bit of reverse appliqué to the leaf.

See page 110 for pattern.

RUFFLED EDGE

This was a fairly early design which may have been inspired by embroidery work.
See page 111 for pattern.

POSY

Be sure to use a variety of shades to bring this bunch of flowers to life.
I was very pleased with the leaves which I feel make a rather ordinary group of flowers much more interesting.

See page 112 for the pattern.

COG WHEELS

This cheerful flower is far easier to sew than you might at first suppose.
It is one which is easy to manipulate to fit into a particular space simply by lengthening,
shortening or pivoting any of the elements to suit your need.

See page 112 for the pattern.

CAULIFLOWER

This is one which my daughter named.
I was completely stuck for a name and asked her.
She didn't even hesitate before saying cauliflower and who's to say she's wrong?

See page 113 for the pattern.

JUNE FLOWER

This design uses one of my favorite "filler" flower shapes.
See page 113 for the pattern.

MUSHROOM DAISY

This is quite a handy design when trying to fill an awkward space because the separate elements in it mean that you can crowd them close or spread them out.

See page 114 for pattern.

LOOPED DAISY

This flower is a variation of the one titled First Flower.
I have included it because it looks different simply through placing the flower heads on a different plant base.
This should start you thinking about how you can mix and match the elements from various flowers to
come up with your own new design. On Goato & Friends, it was first used in the cat block and then modified
to fit a space in the donkey block. I did not use it in CATS but from it developed
yet another variation which is Comet, shown on page 50.

See page 115 for pattern.

DROP FLOWER

It looks a bit sleepy as the flower heads droop down.
This was the first new flower I designed for CATS
and I made it in purples and later in blues and yellows.

See page 116 for the pattern.

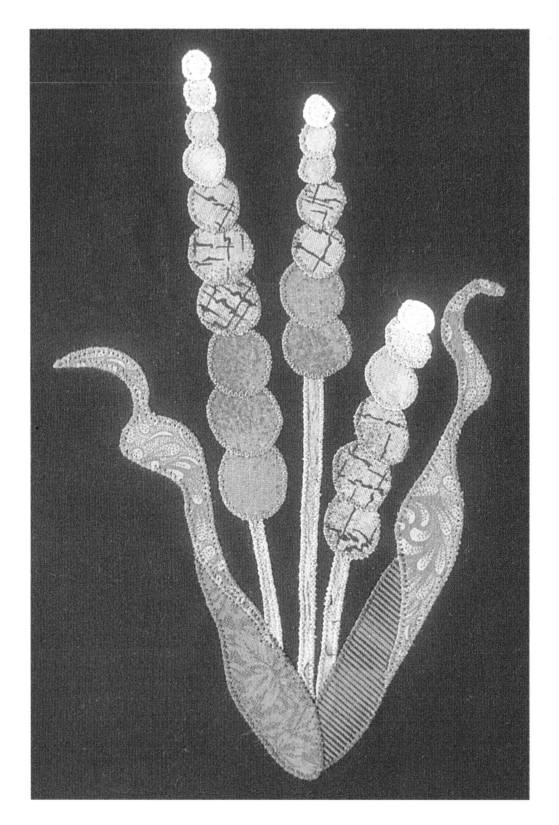

BEAD FLOWER

This was a very early design and a very versatile one because you can add more or take away "beads" to suit your space. It's fun trying to graduate your colours from a previously chosen palette.

See page 116 for the pattern.

BLACK-EYED SUSAN

This is the only flower I have used which has one stem twisting behind another.
It has worked here although without care I think this type of design could look a bit messy.

See page 117 for the pattern.

SNOWBALL FLOWER

This is a fun and easy flower to sew.
It certainly does not resemble any real flower thus inviting you to make it in any colourway.

See page 117 for the pattern.

DAFFODIL

See page 118 for pattern.

BRIAR ROSE

Being another highly stylised flower it is also a very useful one to fill difficult spaces.
You can stretch the flower heads out at somewhat ridiculous angles.

See page 119 for pattern.

LAVA FLOWER

In spite of the slightly vicious name which my daughter gave it,
I think this one sews up looking rather sweet.

See page 120 for the pattern.

COMET

This one came about as a development from the Looped Daisy which can be found on page 42.

See page 120 for the pattern.

SUNRISE

This is yet another that my daughter named but this time
I must confess that the name she gave it was the one which was already in my mind.
In CATS, I gave it a blue "sun" and the "rays" were orange.

See page 121 for the pattern.

PETER'S WINDMILL

Peter drew this one for me and I love it.
It was the last new design for CATS and you can find it along the bottom edge of the quilt.
At the time he drew it he was searching for an old disused windmill
for his own work in the amusement park industry.

See page 121 for the pattern.

FINGER FLOWER

See page 122 for pattern.

LOLLIPOPS

Lollipops come in all colours and so do these flowers. I used this flower twice on both quilts.
In the four times I made it, I used three completely different leaf designs and was equally happy with each of them.

See page 123 for pattern.

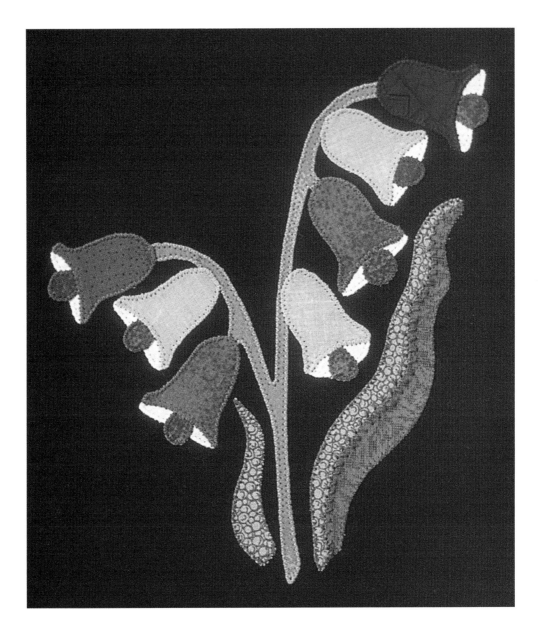

BELL FLOWER

This flower could easily be adapted to suit many situations simply by altering the stem.
To keep it from looking flat, try to use at least three or four different shades for the bells.

See page 124 for the pattern.

IRIS

In the cat block of Goato & Friends, it was made with blues.
When I made it for CATS I used purples. In the example here, Julie Standen used both blue and purple.
It's such a cheerful flower that there are many colours which would work well for it.

See page 125 for the pattern.

PEACE LILY

Sometimes I have been affected by real flowers.
When designing flowers for the cat block in Goato & Friends, I noticed that my white Peace Lily was in bloom.
In the goat block and on CATS I used a red variation.
Julie was not keen to make this flower until I reassured her that they came in red also.

See page 126 for the pattern.

MARIGOLD

When I first designed this for CATS, I made it up in yellows and it reminded me of marigolds.
However, I used it a second time in that quilt but this time used shades of blue
as Julie Standen did in her sample shown here.
You could choose to simplify the leaves for this design.

See page 127 for pattern.

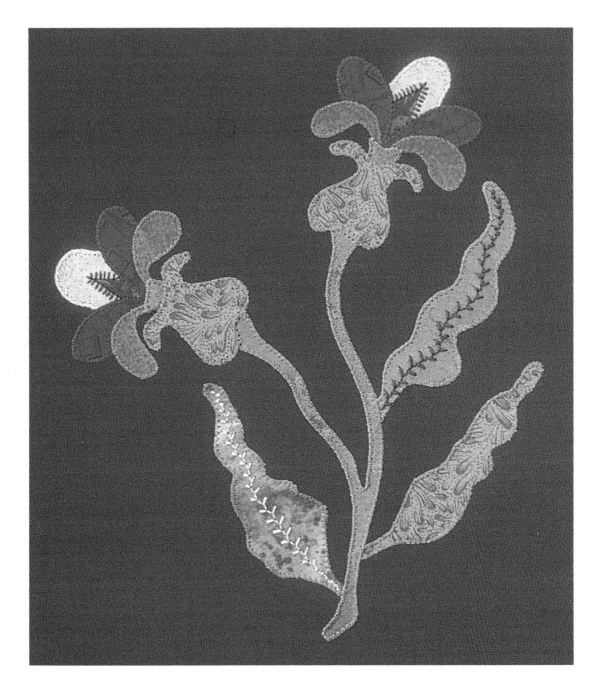

ORCHID

Although this is not in any way based on a real orchid, that is what my daughter,
Eliza named it when she first saw it.

See page 128 for the pattern.

FIRE FLOWER

See page 129 for the pattern.

PUFF BALL

See page 130 for the pattern.

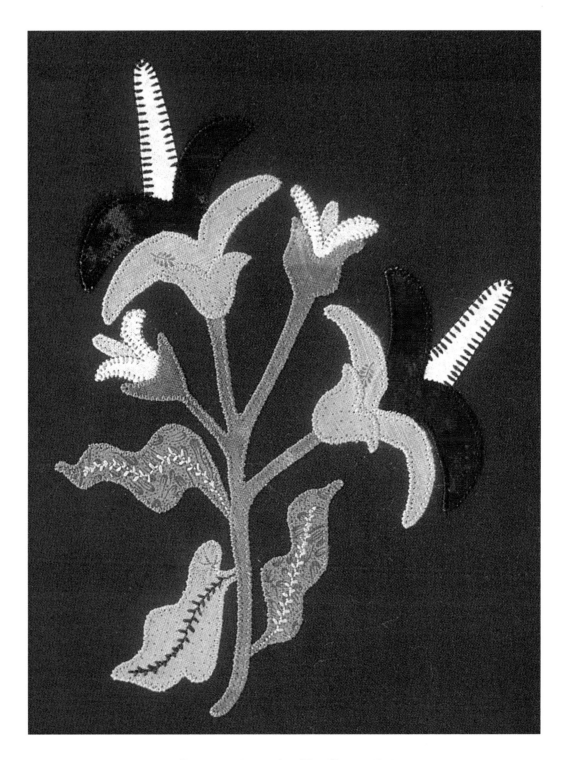

BANANA FLOWER

My daughter Eliza drew and named this flower.
She drew it to fit a space in the donkey block.

See page 131 for the pattern.

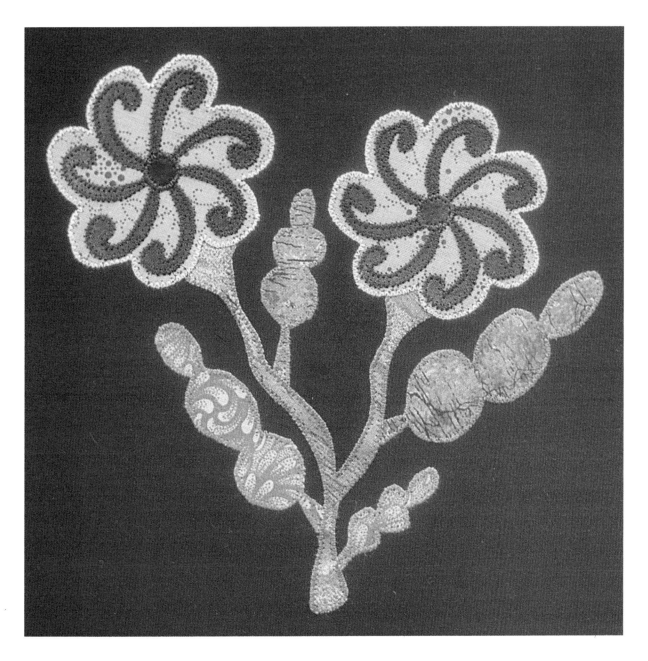

SPIRAL FLOWER

I really do like this flower but have only used it once, near the top of CATS.
There were two reasons why I did not use it again on that quilt.
It is a very dramatic design and I did not really want to repeat it.
Also, the cutting of the centre spirals is a bit fiddly and I thought once was enough!

See page 132 for the pattern.

FOUR SQUARED

See page 133 for the pattern.

PIN CUSHION FLOWER

This one remains a favorite of mine as there is plenty of scope to go a bit wild with colour.

See page 134 for the pattern.

SUNFLOWER

This is a very simplified sunflower and not a very realistic one either.

See page 135 for the pattern.

WINKING SUNFLOWER

The name for this flower comes from Julie Standen's husband.
As Julie was sewing this sample, he said that the flower on the left looked like it was winking.

See page 136 for the pattern.

MELON FLOWER

My daughter named this flower and I can understanding her reasoning
although that was not on my mind when I was drawing it.
For this one the greens are almost more important than the flower colour choice.

See page 137 for the pattern.

POLYANTHUS

This flower is a challenge to make but also a great deal of fun once you figure out the order.

See page 138 for pattern.

SCROLL FLOWER

As this one represents no flower whatsoever, it could be made in any colours.

See page 139 for the pattern.

FRITZ

The first time I made this one for CATS, I left out the centre leaf.
When I made it the second time, I added that leaf and liked it much better.

See page 140 for pattern.

DANDELION

In no way does this look like a real dandelion but that was the image in my mind when I drew it.
The first time I made it for CATS, I did use yellows but by the time
I used it again I must have realised that it looked nothing like a dandelion and used purples.
Maybe by then I saw it as more of a thistle.

See page 141 for the pattern.

WHIRLIGIG

Whirligigs are wonderful, fanciful things that can be any colour
just so long as they will twirl in the wind.

See page 142 for the pattern.

DIVA

When designing so many flowers, there are bound to be some that
appeal less than others on a purely personal basis.
This was one that I designed early on and like less than most.
Having said that, I have used it in both quilts.

See page 143 for the pattern.

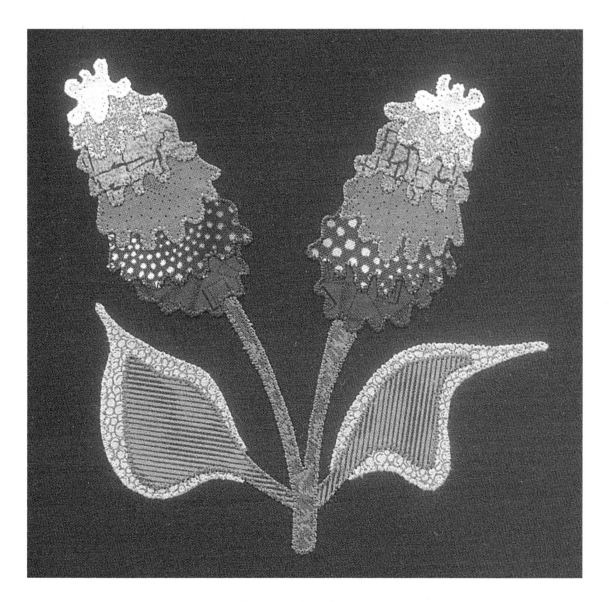

CONE FLOWER

This flower can be fun to shade from a pre-selected palette.
See page 144 for the pattern.

FLAG

See page 145 for the pattern.

VOLVIC

See page 146 for the pattern.

ROSE

See page 147 for the pattern.

LANTERN LIGHTS

See page 148 for the pattern.

MELLOW FLOWER

See page 149 for the pattern.

SPINDLE FLOWERS

Like the previous design, the ones I made for CATS were in purples and oranges.

See page 150 for the pattern.

TIGER BLOOM

This one always struck me as being rather wild and I could never make my mind up
as to whether it came from the dessert or the jungle.

See page 151 for the pattern.

UMBRELLA

My first one of these appears along the top edge of CATS.
At that time it was made with smoothly shaped leaves.
Along the bottom edge of that quilt you can find it with these jagged leaves.
This is another one which for me the greens were more important than the flower colour,
and yes, it looks more like an umbrella than a flower.

See page 152 for the pattern.

DROOPING DAHLIA

Constantly looking for different ideas, I gave this one a flat bottom where the stems and leaves meet.

See page 153 for the pattern.

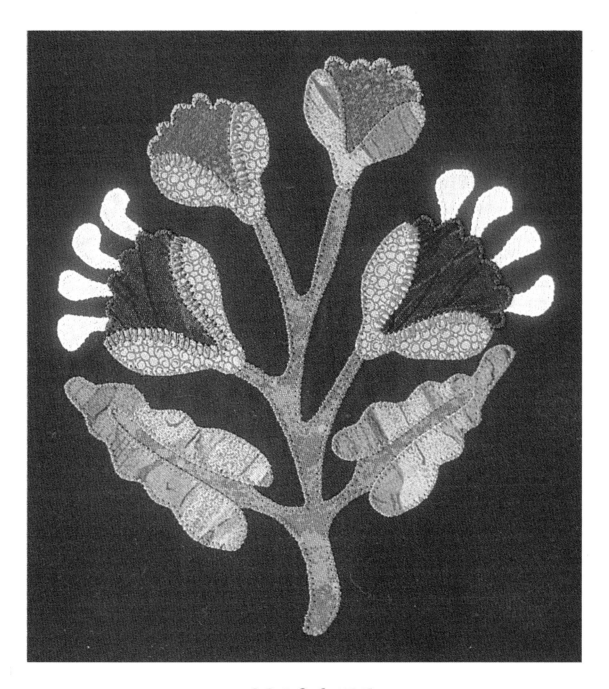

SPROCKET

ee page 154 for the pattern.

TRUMPET FLOWER

This one is easy and pleasing to sew but you could soften some
or all of the points in it to make the stitching even easier.

See page 155 for the pattern.

TRIPOD

Trust a young person to see things simply - my daughter wanted me to call this Three Toes.
We settled on Tripod but now I will always see it as feet with three toes.

See page 156 for the pattern.

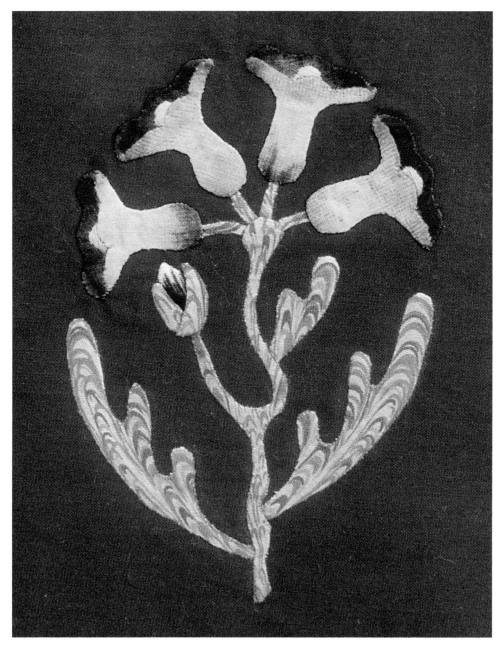

Margaret's Flower
by Margaret Docherty, County Durham, England   1998
Hand Appliqué

The inspiration for the leaves came from a quilt Margaret was working on whilst I was designing flowers.

See page 157 for pattern.

MORE
FLOWERS

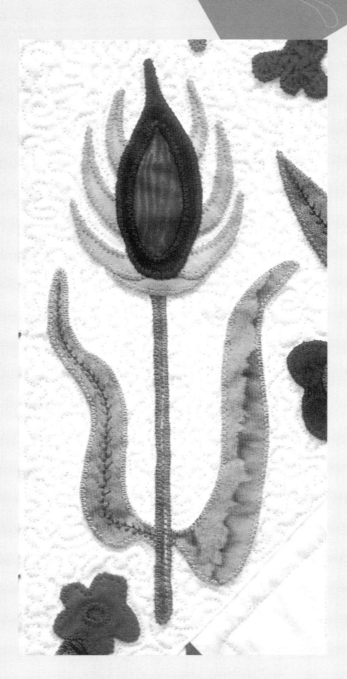

RED HOT POKER

This spear shaped flower was used twice in CATS.
The second version found on the right of the quilt has a frond type of leaf.

See page 158 for the pattern.

MARILYN'S FLOWER

The tiny leaves are a bit of a bother to do but the textural effect makes them worth doing.
See page 158 for the pattern.

LITTLE DAISY

See page 159 for the pattern.

PUFFER FLOWER

This is one which can be easily manipulated to fit a given space.

See page 159 for the pattern.

TOWER FLOWER

This "stacked" flower is a great one for using a variety of shades of one colour.

See page 160 for the pattern.

SPEAR FLOWER

This one was used twice in CATS. In the second variation the leaves were changed to suit the situation.

See page 161 for the pattern.

CUP FLOWER

This one is a good "filler" flower as the shape and size of it can easily be adjusted
by moving, lengthening or shortening the stems.

See page 162 for the pattern.

SLIPPER

Somehow this one reminds me of slippers and I like the wobbly stems.
See page 163 for the pattern.

LITTLE TULIPS

These make super "fillers" as you can move the individual flowers about at will to fill a certain space,
using more or less as needed.

See page 164 for the pattern.

SPRITE

I love the textural difference between the flower head and the many little leaves.

See page 165 for the pattern.

IVY LEAF

This ivy-shaped leaf is another of my favourite leaf shapes and the flower was kept very simple.
See page 166 for the pattern.

SPANNER

See page 167 for the pattern.

FLOWER POWER

BLOWN BONNET

This flower first appeared in the lower left hand section of CATS.
That time it did not have the frilled back section. I prefer it as it is in this second version.

See page 168 for the pattern.

DROPLET

See page 169 for the pattern.

PETER'S FLOWER

FLOWER POWER

POKE FLOWER

SUNDIAL

HOT CROSS BUN FLOWER

LAZY DAISY

CANDLEWICK

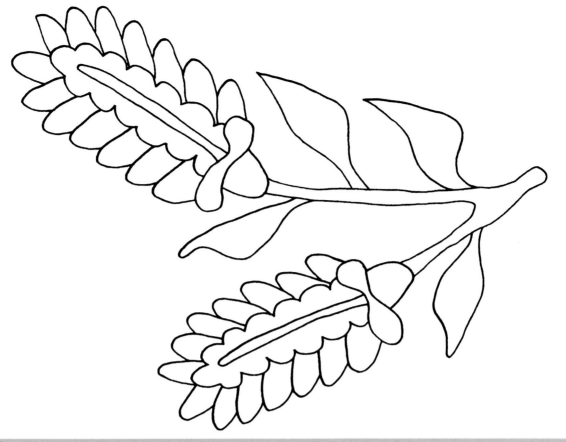

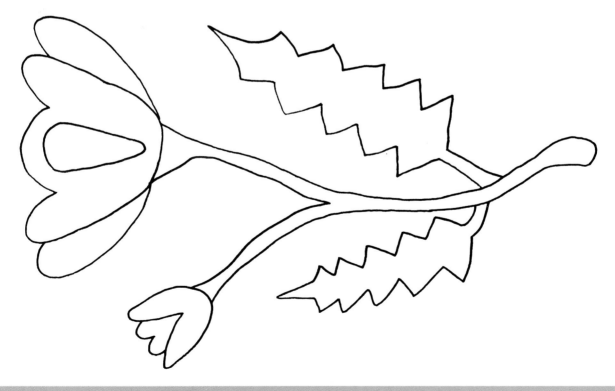

HOUND'S TOOTH

RUFFLED EDGE

POSY

COG WHEELS

CAULIFLOWER

JUNE FLOWER

MUSHROOM DAISY

DROP FLOWER

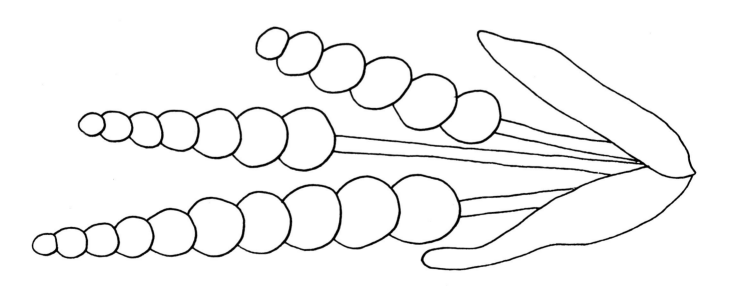

BEAD FLOWER

BLACK-EYED SUSAN

SNOWBALL FLOWER

DAFFODIL

BRIAR ROSE

LAVA FLOWER

COMET

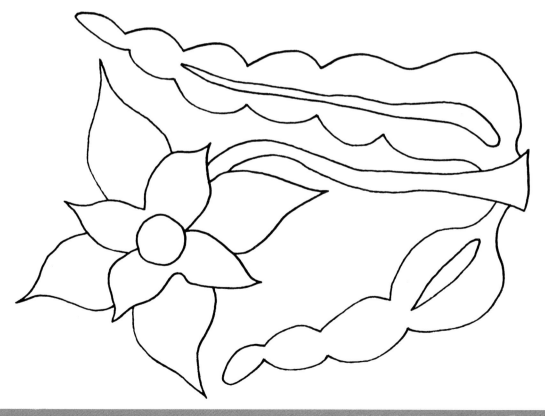

PETER'S WINDMILL

FINGER FLOWER

FLOWER POWER

LOLLIPOPS

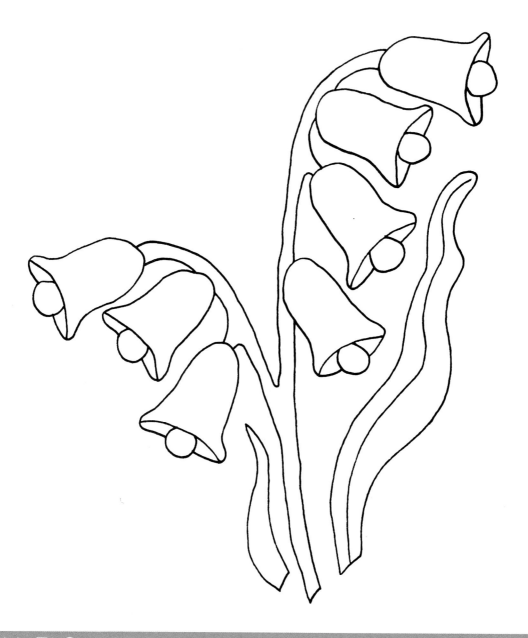

IRIS

PEACE LILY

FLOWER POWER

MARIGOLD

ORCHID

FIRE FLOWER

PUFF BALL

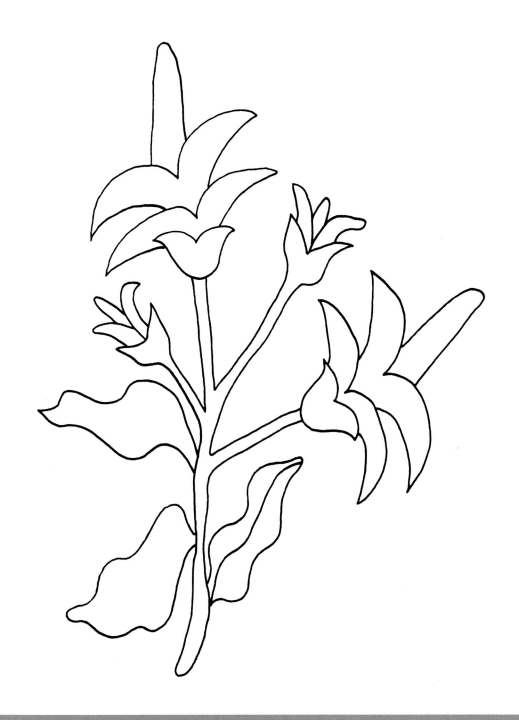

BANANA FLOWER

SPIRAL FLOWER

PIN CUSHION FLOWER

SUNFLOWER

WINKING SUNFLOWER

MELON FLOWER

POLYANTHUS

SCROLL FLOWER

FRITZ

DANDELION

WHIRLIGIG

FLOWER POWER

DIVA

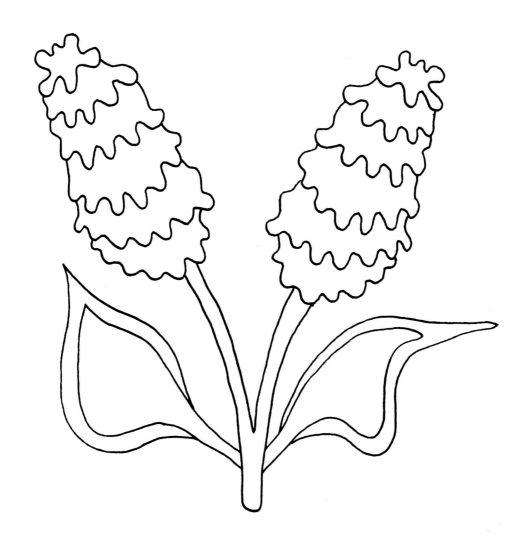

CONE FLOWER

FLAG

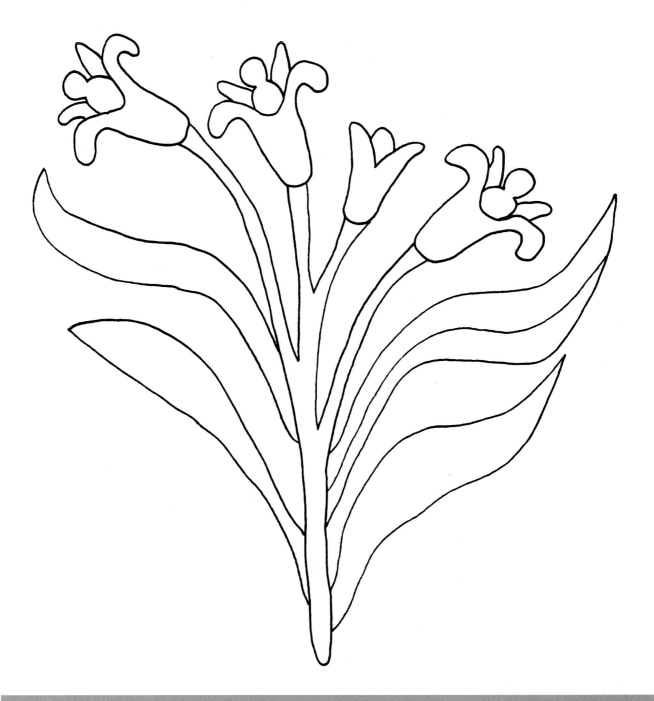

VOLVIC

FLOWER POWER

ROSE

LANTERN LIGHTS

MELLOW FLOWER

SPINDLE FLOWER

TIGER BLOOM

UMBRELLA

FLOWER POWER

DROOPING DAHLIA

TRUMPET FLOWER

TRIPOD

FLOWER POWER

MARGARET'S FLOWER

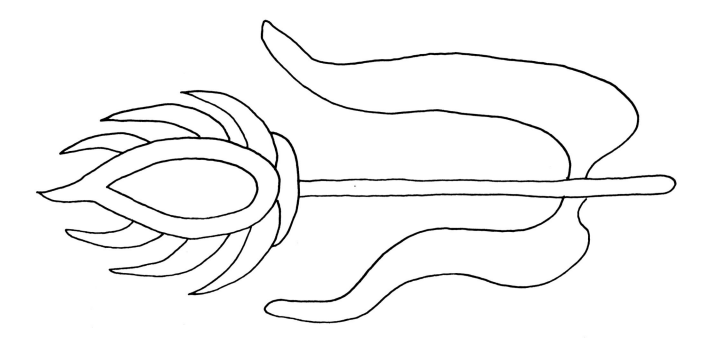

RED HOT POKER

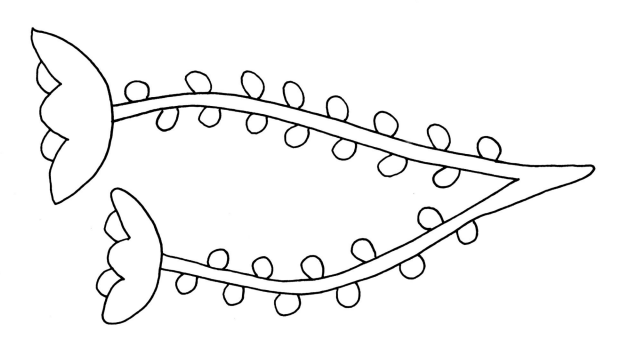

MARILYN'S FLOWER

FLOWER POWER

LITTLE DAISY

PUFFER FLOWER

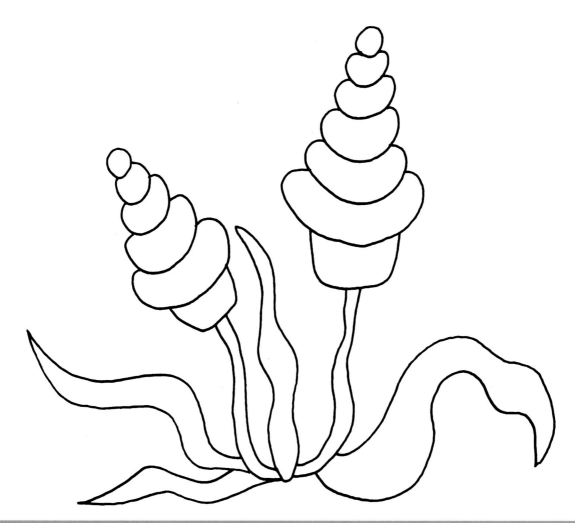

TOWER FLOWER

CUP FLOWER

FLOWER POWER

SLIPPER

LITTLE TULIPS

FLOWER POWER

SPRITE

IVY LEAF

FLOWER POWER

BLOWN BONNET

FLOWER POWER

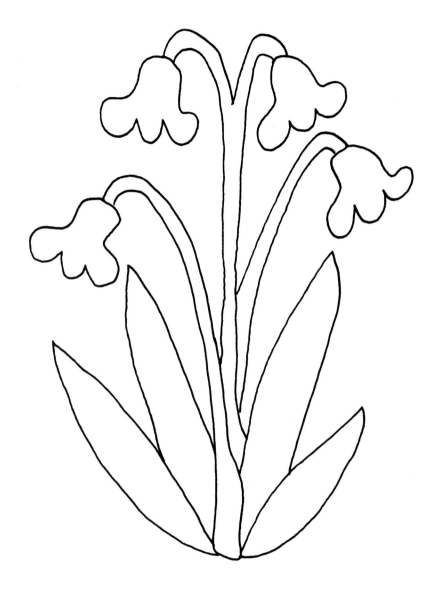

DROPLET

Framed Flowers
by Linda Park, Maryland, USA   1998

In this piece, Linda used the flower design Droplet. She simply cut out the whole design from one fabric and fused it onto a background fabric. Padding was placed under the background before framing.

See page 169 for pattern.

INDEX OF FLOWER PATTERNS

QUILTING VIDEOS by Barbara Barber

"REALLY SHARP PIECING" (video)
This video is a companion to the *Really Sharp Piecing* book, and shows each step in a clearly presented workshop format. Seeing it done makes it easy.

"REALLY SHARP PIECING" (book)
A new method of foundation piecing to create complex quilts with ease and amazing accuracy. This very popular technique was introduced in Barbara's workshop and on the video – the book takes it much further. Step-by-step instructions for 15 quilts with full size patterns. The chapter on deign will lead you to explore endless possibilities. Suitable for all levels.

"COMPLETELY QUILTED"
This video is a complete guide to machine quilting. It covers all the necessary steps as well as hints and tips for achieving beautiful quilting with your sewing machine.

"REALLY QUICK QUILTS"
This video features quick, quality quilts you can give away without feeling you are giving away half your life. New and unusual time saving techniques to produce a quick result. There is no accuracy required with easy "check-points" to assure a quality finish.

"PICTURE THIS" *(New Video)*
A step-by-step guide to Barbara Barber's unique method of machine appliqué. In this video, Barbara demonstrates the basics of machine appliqué for flower designs, enhancing them with machine embroidery. Next, we follow her, step-by-step and learn how she creates her amazingly realistic animals, a technique that can be applied to many other subjects.

These videos have been professionally produced with excellent close-ups and are available from:

PB Publications
Ramridge Dene, Weyhill, Andover, Hants SP11 0QP UK   *Tel: 01264 772465*

"DESIGNER QUILTING BY HAND & MACHINE"
In this video Margaret Docherty joins Barbara to take your quilting beyond ordinary. Together they explore quilting patterns, techniques and encourage you to design your own.

Available from:
Glover Publications, Relly Farm, Broom Lane, Broom Park, Durham DH7 7RJ UK